Scooters

BY **THOMAS STREISSGUTH**

BELLWETHER MEDIA · MINNEAPOLIS, MN

Are you ready to take it to the extreme?
Torque books thrust you into the action-packed
world of sports, vehicles, and adventure.
These books may include dirt, smoke, fire, and
dangerous stunts.
WARNING: Read at your own risk.

Library of Congress Cataloging-in-Publication Data

Streissguth, Thomas, 1958–
  Scooters / by Thomas Streissguth.
      p. cm. – (Torque–motorcycles)
  Summary: "Full color photography accompanies engaging information about Scooters.
The combination of high-interest subject matter and light text is intended for students in
grades 3 through 7"–Provided by publisher.
  Includes bibliographical references and index.
  ISBN-13: 978-1-60014-158-4 (hardcover : alk. paper)
  ISBN-10: 1-60014-158-7 (hardcover : alk. paper)
  1. Motor scooters–Juvenile literature. I. Title.

  TL450.S77 2008
  629.227'5–dc22   2007040748

This edition first published in 2008 by Bellwether Media.

CONTENTS

WHAT IS A SCOOTER?

A scooter is a unique, motorized street vehicle. It is simple to operate, comfortable and fun to ride, and it gets great **gas mileage**. It also costs less than most cars and motorcycles. It's not hard to see why scooters are one of the most popular forms of **urban** transportation on the planet.

The first scooters were made in Italy in the 1950s. The designers wanted a low-cost, motorized street vehicle. Motorized bicycles had been around since the late 1800s. Those bikes were noisy to operate and uncomfortable to ride.

The first real scooter wasn't just another motorized bicycle. It was a totally new invention. It had small wheels and a big, comfortable seat. It also had a wide, low **footboard**. This **"step-through" design** made it easy for anyone to get on and off. It was an instant hit.

FAST FACT

THE FIRST SCOOTER WAS THE VESPA. THE WORD VESPA MEANS "WASP" IN ITALIAN. THE ITALIAN DESIGNERS THOUGHT IT LOOKED AND MOVED LIKE A SLEEK, STREAMLINED WASP. TODAY THERE ARE MANY OTHER POPULAR SCOOTER MAKERS, INCLUDING APRILIA AND HONDA. HOWEVER, THE MOST FAMOUS SCOOTER ON THE PLANET IS STILL THE VESPA.

FAST FACT

THE FIRST SCOOTERS WERE DESIGNED JUST AFTER WORLD WAR II. ITALIAN ROADS HAD BEEN HEAVILY DAMAGED IN THE WAR. THE DESIGNERS WANTED A SMALL VEHICLE THAT COULD EASILY NAVIGATE THE DAMAGED ROADS.

Many scooters come with small engines. They range in size between 49 and 100 **cubic centimeters** (cc). The top speed of most scooters is about 40 miles (64 kilometers) per hour. Some sport models have engines as large as 700cc. Larger engines can go 55 miles (88.5 kilometers) per hour or even faster. Most scooters can travel 120 miles (193 kilometers) on one gallon (3.8 liters) of gas.

Scooters are fun and easy to ride. A simple switch or button starts the engine. The frame is lightweight and stable. The scooterist can maneuver easily. The brakes and throttle are in easy reach on the handlebar. The wide front frame blocks street dirt and dust from being sprayed up onto the rider.

Like the driver of any vehicle, a scooterist must pay attention to safety. Scooterists should wear helmets. They should also follow all the rules of the road.

SCOOTERS
IN ACTION

A scooter fan today can choose from many models. The classic step-through design is still the most popular. Sport versions have larger wheels and bigger, more powerful engines. High-powered electric scooters run on battery power instead of fuel. Other choices include off-road scooters, pickup scooters, and 3-wheel utility scooters.

FAST FACT

THE MOPED IS AN EVEN SMALLER MOTORIZED STREET VEHICLE WITH AN ENGINE SIZE OF 49 CUBIC CENTIMETERS OR SMALLER. THEY LOOK LIKE SMALL MOTORCYCLES WITHOUT THE STEP-THROUGH DESIGN OF SCOOTERS.

Scooters can also be used for work. They are great for urban delivery jobs. Drivers can easily navigate narrow streets and alleys. Most scooters fit in bike racks, so finding a parking space is never a problem. The big seat has room for bulky items or an additional passenger. Scooters are even used as taxis in some countries. Need a ride?

GLOSSARY

cubic centimeters–a measurement of engine size; larger engines produce more power than smaller engines.

footboard–a platform where the driver rests his or her feet

gas mileage–the amount of gas used for every mile traveled

step-through design–the classic scooter design with the low, flat footboard; this allows the rider to board by stepping through an open space in the middle of the vehicle.

urban–having to do with city life

TO LEARN MORE

AT THE LIBRARY

Pupeza, Lori Kinstad. *Scooters: The Ultimate Motorcycles.* Edina, Minn.: Abdo, 1998.

Streissguth, Thomas. *Standard Motorcycles.* Minneapolis, Minn.: Bellwether, 2008.

ON THE WEB

Learning more about motorcycles is as easy as 1, 2, 3.

1. Go to www.factsurfer.com

2. Enter "motorcycles" into search box.

3. Click the "Surf" button and you will see a list of related web sites.

With factsurfer.com, finding more information is just a click away.

INDEX

The images in this book are reproduced through the courtesy of: Yamaha Motor Corporation, cover, pp. 5, 10-11, 16, 18; pbpgalleries/Alamy, pp. 6-7; Steven Miric, p. 9; AFP/Getty Images, p. 12; Juan Martinez, p. 13; Lena Granefelt, p. 14; American Honda Motor Co., p. 19; Peter Treanor/Alamy, p. 20.